Bad Dreams of a Hungry Dog

Poems of Spiritual Odyssey and A Quest For Enlightenment

Jere Truer

Bad Dreams of a Hungry Dog
Poems of Spiritual Odyssey and A Quest For Enlightenment
Copyright © 2021 by Jere Truer

Library of Congress Control Number: 2021902729
ISBN-13: Paperback: 978-1-64749-370-7
           ePub: 978-1-64749-369-1

All rights reserved. No part of this publication may be reproduced, distributed, or transmitted in any form or by any means, including photocopying, recording, or other electronic or mechanical methods, without the prior written permission of the publisher or author, except in the case of brief quotations embodied in critical reviews and certain other noncommercial uses permitted by copyright law.

Although every precaution has been taken to verify the accuracy of the information contained herein, the author and publisher assume no responsibility for any errors or omissions.No liability is assumed for damages that may result from the use of information contained within.

Printed in the United States of America

GoToPublish LLC
1-888-337-1724
www.gotopublish.com
info@gotopublish.com

Jere Truer
919 East 24th Place
Yuma, AZ 85365
Ph: 612-916-9833
jeretruer@gmail.com

ACKNOWLEDGMENTS

Many of these poems have been published in previous revisions in several small press literary journals which sadly have closed up shop. Among them are Germination in Canada, Sidewalks in Minnesota, InRoads in Minnesota, and Talking Stick in Minnesota.

I have published most of these poems online on my own site on Facebook, "An Unfinished Conversation". Many have appeared in the online journals Martin Lake and Lawless Poetry.

I wish to thank John Huber who got me first turned onto poetry in 1971 as a sophomore at what is now Ridgewater Community College. I am indebted to the late John Mitchell who was my advisor, provocateur, and mentor at Augsburg College.

I received tremendous support, feedback, and friendship from The Bedford Poets. Among them are Thomas R. Smith, John Krumberger, Daniel Thomas, Daniel Bachhuber, Eric Austin, Jane Graham George, Diane Jarvenpa, Scott King, Roger Parrish, and Maureen Skelly.

Because this is a book of my spiritual odyssey, my teachers and guides, many of them now deceased, are Alfred Sevig, Floyd Lien, Cal Appleby, Susan Veiera, Miriam Pew, Fred Mueller, and the healer who uttered to me during a healing session thirty years ago, "The path to enlightenment is like the bad dream of a hungry dog". His name is Bill Torvund.

I have been blessed with many like-minded friends who accompanied me, for at least a little while. We have had many soul-searching conversations over the years which got mulled over and turned into poems. These friends are Robert Roggeveen, Jeffery Grundtner, Greg Ruud, Fannella Collins, Julie Tallard Johnson, my late wife Tamara Chaney Truer, and my current wife Monica Schurtz Truer.

I also want to acknowledge the Yuma Writers Consortium who welcomed me into their midst in the autumn of 2016 as a newly transplanted Yuman being after moving from my long-term home in Minneapolis and shorter term home in Colorado. They are too numerous and fluid to name individually but the leaders are Dana Mann-Chipkin and Mark Galaga.

And, of course, I thank my publisher and editors at Austin Macauley.

EGYPT

Jere Truer

ANOTHER MAN WATCHING

A great storm sweeps across the north
Over the mountains down to the rivers
And along the lower Colorado where I live,
Where it turns vicious-- hurling dust and sand,
Overturning whatever is not rooted or fastened.

Because I am mired in politics as of late--
Because whenever the president opens a Bible
There is trouble—this maelstrom feels personal
With everything beloved by me put on the short list
For annihilation. And people like me are in the way.

And yea, though the warmongers pray
To a vengeful god to sweep clean the world
Of the soft-hearted, the sentimental, the poets

And absent minded dreamers: the lovers;
My prayers are to the One who welcomes

The windblown and dispossessed, wanderers
Who have broken their vows a thousand times.
Listen, I know I am useless to the Regime
Because I fall and weep. But in falling and rolling,
I am more resilient, more stubborn than any ill wind.

And I refuse to despair.

DIGGING IN THE GROUND

The sharp scratchy sound of a spade
Opening a grave cannot be mistaken—
An old, old sound, unsettling and sad.
Earlier today I read from a man in Paris

As he mentioned Chagall, Baudelaire,
And Sartre in one breath. Comfort
Followed by loneliness fell over me.
I resonate not to the current but the ancient.

You and I have known the old decadence
And beauty, the patina of history
Burnishing our old relics and art.
But knowledge borne of history seems lost:

Now relegated to history itself and memory
Inconveniences the seamless, efficient
Upload of an idiot future without mirrors.
There are no paintings—only posters—

And no sculpture—only molded tchotchkes.
The luxuriant boredom, delicious ennui,
Which births dreams and revolutions
Drowns in the foaming sea of constant

Stimulation and spontaneous amnesia.
And I, too, am forgotten and forget myself.
But I regret to tell you I am too real
To myself, and I hear the spade take the earth.

I hear a mechanical voice tell me
I do not belong here anymore. It may be right.
I belong no more to the manufactured,
The entertained and distracted.

And so I go toward the eternal, to the high winds
Coursing over this sacred Earth, over old stones,
Across the moors, through the pipes and drum beats,
Following the voices of my ancestors.

I have tried all my life to sing their song.

A NIGHT LIKE THIS

The sky tonight is so gentle

And the fat lady has not begun her song,
Although standing on the prow of the ship
Of state.

Has anyone informed the president
That the beginning of the beginning
Of the swan song is about to be sung?

Perhaps this was the plan all along.
You read the great Greek tragedies, no?
The chorus always knows.

I have been listening

As have you

And that is why we are each wide
Awake at 2:07 on a Saturday morning.

I am too exhausted to detail the horrors
Of history and how they become
The horrors of today.

But what I really wanted to say is
That we were born for times like these
Or else we would have not been born at all.

But that is not it either.
I was born for a night like this:
The sky so gentle,

The moon, waning from full,
Drifts above us, full of wandering stars.
Dreams float over bedrooms

Looking for a way to get in.

BORN UNDER THE SIGN OF PLUTO

I was born under the sign of Pluto
Five years after it was discovered
Making its strange course along the edges
At the perimeter of our solar system.
A chunk of odd-shaped and frozen rock,
Reduced and demoted as of late from the club
Of fellow planets. But it is only our denial.
We do not tolerate the abductor, the god of rape
Who steals young women like Persephone,
Holding them captive till a bargain is reached.

He is father to plutonium and the nuclear age.
All of us born after 1947 have the destruction
Of Earth in our DNA. Born a millennium later
Than expected by the old knowers, he truly is
The dark twin to Christ. I had a slight crush
On a pretty seminarian once. I teased her, asking
How does the scatological pertain to eschatology.
She hid her blush, changed the subject, and
Ignored me forever after that. But now I know
That this is the time of the world turned to shit.

As I write these lines, we are two decades
Into the Twenty-first Century. My country
Is ruled by a mad despot among other mad despots.
How to we presume a future? How shall we plan
For anything? Perhaps this is what it means
To be in the grip of Pluto, what it means when young
Men turn themselves into bombs, taking out
Hundreds when they explode, resurrecting hell
To the surface of the earth and plunging all beauty
Far, far beneath the ground.

I do not like speaking these words.
They make me sick and disturb my sleep.
My name may have something to do
With how I write jeremiads, furthermore I am

Really christened Jerome, my baptismal name.
And that early prophet was not at all sanguine
Would that I could content myself with writing
Words to entertain a daydreaming young girl
Or comfort an old man on a wintry night.
But I am not so wise, nor can I find the words,
And I pray as well as curse on my muttering way.

RENUNCIATIONS

RENUNCIATION I

Another crossroad finds itself beneath my feet.
How many does that make now? Too many, perhaps.
Yet here I pause, here I stand, uncertain for the first time

In my sometimes too deliberate life about where to go,
What to do. Where I am is a good place, and in myself
I feel happy. Yet the world still begs something else.

Everywhere I look I see mirrors with no reflection.
People stand before them screaming they cannot see.
No one can hear, either, for the cacophony of broadcast

Voices and exploding bombs. But the mirrors,
The mirrors disturb me more. Yes, there are images,
Faces of something not quite human.

But it is my job to clean the glass no more.
You can peer into the glass to seek your reflection
Better yet--to look through it, to see beyond,

To see what lives outside. But do not expect the glass
To tell you anything about yourself. Like Snow White's
Witch, you may not like what it shows you.

After a lifetime spent in translating and interpreting,
I go now to know what I truly resemble,
To re-assemble a vision from long ago, before

The nets of the human world ensnared me,
Hoisting me up beyond myself into an actor's
Role portraying who I was supposed to be.

There is only one glass, one mirror, one lens
For me to look through now—the one through
Which I may see the ancient world

And the visage of my King.

RENUNCIATION II

The end of day finds me taking account:
But is it in what I have had or lost or squandered?
Or in what I have done, not done, or regretted?
Or is it something else which needs accounting for?

I have owned four houses but had many homes,
Most not more than a hundred miles away
From where I was born. But ventured four times
Into the wilderness of marriage, wandered
The mountains down to the desert with wife
Number four, collecting four step-children.
And yet there was a letting go at every turn.

We may choose what we collect along the way.
We may choose where we go, and how far,
But often not our traveling companions
Nor when it is we must say goodbye.
And to spare myself or protect my mask,
I took up the habit of renunciation—
Of refusing on ethical grounds.

When I was a small child needing maternal succor,
My mother crawled into the crib instead.
I had to renounce her and renounce my own need.

When I fell in love as a young man
With women unsuitable to my mother,
I could stand her jealous cries
And scorned rebukes no longer.

I renounced those whom I loved
And renounced myself thereby,
"Binding with briars my joys and desires".

Bad Dreams of a Hungry Dog

My last and current wife could have been
My first and only. But I had to break her heart
And mine, exiled for forty years instead.

And so, friends, I account for this.
I own what I have and have done what I did.
I could have had so much more.
And if I had what I truly desired,
I would need less of all the rest.

(quote by William Blake)

THE DEATH OF ME / RENUNCIATION III

As my sixtieth year approached
I began planning for my death.
I had no goal nor strategy in mind
Other than that I could see it from there.

So it was fitting I should wake up dead
Two days past my birthday, or
To be precise, just back from the dead.
Twice. Twice I died on the operating table.

I do not remember it: I was dead.
When I came back, several doctors surrounded
My hospital bed. *Do you feel this?*
Feel what? *Or can you feel that?*

I used to play a game when much younger
Where I was blind or wheelchair bound.
At least I could now see, but in my habitual
Renunciation, I had now to renounce my legs.

Surgeons had carved into my spine
To clean out the septic sac of pus
Squeezing the life out of my spinal cord
And ultimately out of me.

The side door of the theatre was left open.
It was an easy out, a get out of life free card.
A quick slip away, no muss or fuss.
Nor much mystery for people to ponder.

I paid my eldest daughter a visit one night
During my intoxicated equivocation
While my ravaged body lay anesthetized
With the query: to stay or go.

To be or not to be, to stay awake and alive,
To suffer anxiety, doubt, pain, and guilt.
Or choose unconsciousness and death,
The milky dream of the unborn.

2

Ah yes, I remember that! The choice made
From the ethers as I consulted Doctor Meredith,
Whoever that is. My guardian angel?
I called out to him years ago while awakening.

He whom I have never seen except glimpsed
From the corners of my eyes, darting by.
He whose voice, not unlike my own,
Perceived in the din and cacophony,

My name called from far away
Amid the echoes of cheers from Heaven
When we each make our confounding kenosis,
Gaining extra credit on our karmic transcript.

None of us must be here, but we are beloved
Even more for the confusion and the courage.
So how is it we walk about lonely and orphaned
Praying for rescue and return.

All this I awoke to in my sixtieth year
In a hospital bed in a paralyzed body.
I could not keep from weeping.
No, I could not keep from weeping.

3

When a body is fully alive in youth,
The soul lies dreaming till jolted awake
By some foolish maneuver meant to impress.
But we forget in our impetuousness

That flight and weightlessness got left behind
In the task of incarnation. Then to sleep we go
Till we wake up much older with the dead
Weight of an uncooperative body.

My poor body, and it was a good one—
Strong, enduring, flexible as I aged—
Now seeming half dead, at least heavy
And numb, demanded full attention

From my soul, which now did the heavy
Lifting, lugging me through my life
But not without complaint or self-pity.
Unlike my body which did it joyfully.

Soul must now learn a new, foreign dance
Of clapping its hands, stomping its feet,
Singing and louder singing for every rip
And tear in its mortal frame.

4

When half dead, one has twice a choice:
To finish it and wholly die, or become twice
Alive. I chose the latter and gave away
Two items for every one I kept.

Death and loss held no mortgage on my soul.
I cut the ropes which bound my joy and grief,
Renouncing all the temporary shames
In favor of eternal release.

Yes, and I renounced my easy out.
But remaining meant breaking all the rules
Except those of the heart. I anticipated her
Who had not yet arrived, but was arriving yet.

ESCHATOLOGY

MORNING'S BLESSING

From my tiny ramshackle
Shrine I look out
Across my small city,
Its broken promises.

There is poverty here,
As well as confusion and sadness.
There are also singers,
Artists, and such.

Scoundrels abide
As do anonymous saints.
Angels pass by in rags,
Pushing grocery carts.

I hear advice to see only
The good and bountiful I desire.
But if we cannot bless what exists,
Then curses surely follow us.

REMINDING THE DRAGON

I have made a little shrine,
Not to myself
But to the divine mystery
For which I have no answer.

A gong from Tibet hangs
In the small doorway
And I meditate within,
Sitting on a camping chair.

I wake up frightened
And confused some days.
I sit looking out,
Then ring the gong when done.

An old story tells of a monk
Who rang a gong every day
To remind the dragon
Not to destroy the village.

Who am I?
I am not monk
And have no temple.
I do what I can.

SABBATH

At the end of a long week
At the end of a long month
At the end of a long year
Amid a long decade
Of endless commerce and campaign,
Friends, I am exhausted.

Today is Saturday, Sabado,
The Seventh Day when it is time
To let be whatever has been toiled over,
To let stand whatever has been built,
However unfinished. The food
On the stove? Let it cool.

The world we have is left unfinished,
Certainly imperiled and vulnerable
To millions of onslaughts.
Ramparts have been abandoned,
The generals drunk, the king in bed
With another kingdom's queen.

When has this ever not been the case?
The reasons for taking up arms
Or rushing to the marketplace
Buzz through the air like gnats,
Endlessly. If you hear only silence
From me as I near the end

Of the Sixth Day of my life,
Know I am not dead
Nor at market, nor battlefield.
You will find me in the desert wind
Where timeless music sounds
Trying to get some needed rest.

FACING NORTH

Today I greet the day as I always do—
Facing north from my front porch,
Mountains in the distance, swaying palms
In the foreground, serene fields beyond--
With gratitude for simply being here
Regardless how hard the being.

Doves, blue jays, and sparrows
Argue like the Greek fisherman I met
Back in Naxos over coffee at dawn:
Braggadocious, territorial, yet sublime
From high above on their wires.
The music of dissonance and consonance.

When I am beset with the evil humans do,
Which is often and a lot, I remember
Evil has its home only in the human
Heart. The rest of Creation is pure
In its orderliness and consequence.
The order of the day: to reform the heart.

A MEDITATION IN THE CORNER

The bird of paradise tree was dying
At the top--the blossoms falling,
Shriveling, while the greenery browned
And withered on the dry brittle branches.
All I could do to save it was cut off
What was dead and water the rest.
Now it is a thriving, low-lying bush.

The flowers vibrant red, orange, and yellow--
Upheld and proud, like Kabbalah
Sephiroth—flames of the ten kingdoms
But lying close to the earth.
What does this tell us?
That the Tree of Life is tired of heaven
And longs once again for its Mother?

Yes, paradise is here, if we can see.
Forget about all this leaping about,
Insisting on spiritual perfection elsewhere.
The best thing is to be a kind human being.
Or has earth's nature taught you nothing?
But look at me: I wore the dunce cap
In the corner till just yesterday.

AMAZON BURNING

As a child I wondered,
Why am I me?
It is not self-pity as in 'why me'.
It is in how the luck of the draw
Or God sorts us out into lives.
And I am stuck with my tiny one.

And garbage also fascinated me
In terms of where 'does it go?'
I calculated one Sunday how much paper
Went into printing the Sunday Tribune
In Minneapolis: you don't want to know.
But decay also intrigues me, inspires me
Even—all those old books and clothes
And toys and implements in thrift store
Windows beckoning us to care.

And now we hear of the Amazon Rainforest
Burning, and California, too, and God knows
Where else. Is the whole world disposable?
And, by extension, are we? And can we,
In our little lives, put out the all-consuming fire
Which tells us we are nothing but fuel?

We must decide that we do indeed matter
For we are made of matter, and matter
Matters. The humble stuff of our lives
And the stuff of indigenous forest dwellers
Matters as much as the symphonies of Beethoven
Or the stock portfolios of Wall Street bankers
Or the Libraries of Congress or books of the Bible.

Oh, yes, it does. And every little gesture
Of salvation saves the whole, as the proverb

Goes: save a life—whatever form that life,
And save the world. So, I will arise now
To praise this earth-bound life around me
And plant a tree, or two, or more.

WHAT THE EARTH DID NOT SAY

I had my talk
With the great Earth being
This morning
As I always try to do.

But we did not talk
But just wept and wept.
No words to say:
Just weeping and more weeping.

PRAISE FOR THE MOTHER

Every morning from my perch outside
I call to Mother Gaia just like the birds do,
From their aeries high above. I say blessings
And gratitude for the endless bounty
Of every possible thing—

These bodies which serve us
Freely without complaint,
These breezes which cool us,
As well as fire and all things consumed
By us, by the fires inside us.

I crash about on this Earth
As a drunk at three in the morning
Trying come home quietly.
What do I give her but my tears,
My griefs and utter helplessness.

I owe her my life, and she will take it
As easily as she gave it--swiftly.
And she will generously give it again.
But remember, it is all on loan.
What can I say but thank you!

I look down at my hands in my lap,
And at my dirty feet. Such a blessing
To have this worn out body bear me.
It would be a shame to be adrift
In the ethers as a rootless soul.

PICKING UP SHIT

Beneath the hot sun of midday
On my deserted desert yard
I went out to pick up dried dog dung
Accumulated over two weeks of neglect.
Dingo, the Australian cattle dog
Who shares our home with us,
Poops very politely and courteously
In only a certain area.
This makes the unpleasant job
Easier and quicker.
I will not Tom Sawyer you
Into enthusiasm for poop scooping,
And you may be appalled
At my method: I use bare fingers.
The little turds get confused into gravel
And only digits can extricate them.

Despair and shame dog me
About my own, and our collective,
Alienation from the natural world.
This humble, humbling but not humiliating
Reach into fecundity compensates
For that. And furthermore, it is dust—
Holy dust used to create us long ago--
That I use to cleanse my fingers.

FROM A SEEDED ASH

For nearly twenty years
I lived below a hundred year-
Old seeded ash tree.
A grandmother from the time
Before my city was a city,
Before my home was a home,
From long before my birth.

We would talk nearly daily
Once I learned to listen to her.
I could feel how her roots below
Reached out far across the earth
And loved us enough to let us
Dwell beneath her sheltering boughs.
And I came to know

That those same boughs were roots,
As well--roots that reached
Up into the heavens
As far down as the lower roots
Reached into earth.
Leaning upon her, I could feel
The currents of heaven

In its marriage to earth.

THISTLE

Thistles must thrive on dog piss.
They must, for all summer my dog
Showered the ankle-high David,
Standing defiant with its small
But significant protestations.
I had to admire it and tend it
Till it grew to my chest.

Had I pulled it out,
Condemning it to ignominy
In the compost of the damned,
Then what?
Would I be one who allows
No prickliness or shadow
In the Garden?

No, I nurtured a stalk
To tower into the clouds
Which a wise-assed kid can climb
While he plans to steal
Back the treasure
Stolen from his father.
And that belongs to him.

THE MATCH

The weeds in the north Sonoran Desert
Are tough sons of bitches. Their pricks
Stick into and vex my hands for days
When I pull them out bare-handed.

Their stubborn, deep roots go down
All the way to the center of the Earth.
I hear their curses at me as I curse them
With language to make the devil blush.

Deliberate is their place in the kingdom,
Ruffians among many genteel florae.
In protecting my bougainvillea and sage,
And birds of paradise plants, I fight them.

No one wins this match, nor should they.
Whatever meager achievements I made,
I credit my stubble born rages and refusals.
And I myself am no hothouse orchid either.

Sometimes bare knuckled and pugnacious,
Noxious and obnoxious, like my brother weeds.
Yet I cannot, nor will I, kill them, ever.
I keep slugging them back out of respect.

FLIES

Let us all agree to forgive
Flies for being flies.
Yes, their larval stage repels us
But what newborn creature
Does not appetize or nauseate?

Yes, they crawl all over shit
And other rotting things,
Tracking their filthy feet,
Contaminating everything
Everywhere from every place.

Right now, three are slurping
Microscopic things off my skin.
They are simply doing their jobs
Just as we justify our jobs doing
What they do, but on a larger scale.

A DANCE WITH COCKROACH

While pacing the floor these troubled times
When all politic has become absurd,
When the winds carry the ashes and soot
Of half the world on fire,
When mold spores borne on other breezes
From the other half of the world
Sinking and rotting in deluge,
And comforting words reek of denial,
It is difficult not to side with the devil
In his wager against human worth.

I confess to having these bleak fantasies,
And I know that I am not alone in this dark.
Know that plans for our eradication
Are rolling out the subbasements
Of the Capitols and the Pentagon.
Accounts and actuarials do not balance
On the worth of our souls in the devil's books.
And it remains whether we will ultimately
Cash out, having agreed to be worth only
What the markets of the world allow.

But I would rather be here than
To have missed out on love and chocolate,
Vivaldi and Bob Dylan, and the gratitude
Only a drunk feels having survived the night.
I have been to hell a few times, refused the Dark Lord,
And learned, finally, to play music down there.
When the final solution to our existence comes,
I plan to be like the poisoned cockroach
In my kitchen years ago who danced up and down
My leg till he finally, with a smile, succumbed.

HOW THE LORD LETS US LIVE

It is just past noon on a Saturday.
The day has an elasticity about it
Which can accommodate many spirits
Within the capacious sunny breeze.
My confreres half a world away huddle
In their windwrecked snowladen houses.

And a note from a friend up there
Carries a drifting memory from long ago
When I shivered at a bus stop in Minneapolis
While trying to protect a painting I had done.
It was of a cold woman, barefoot on a cliff,
Enshrouded in a dark green cloak.

A pockmarked, whiskey perfumed man
Desperately tried to light a cigarette,
Cupping his trembling frozen hands
Around the fragile flame of his match.
He looked up at me, then the painting,
Then said, "I have seen her many times".

Something in me woke up startled and messy.
A fascination with the gifts borne by beggars--
The downtrodden, the avoided and forgotten—
Was born then that guided me to the Lamed
Vov. They are the angels dressed down
In charity house rags who wander the earth.

They are sent out each day by God
Into our world seeking kindness and mercy.
We know too well how this world works.
We are not surprised to know of their oppression.
We hear these stories every day and we still
Ignore them when they approach.

At day's end, God hears their stories
As they drink wine around the fire.
Only one tale of kindness or mercy
Is enough for the Lord to let us live
One more day. But upon hearing nothing,
The Lord would clap his hands. It would be over.

It would all be over. Completely.
Do I remember The Void before the Breath?
Perhaps. Or when God was born?
Perhaps. Are we each of us the Lamed Vov?
Perhaps. And so this day is blessed
As the whole world passes through my hands

And I hold onto nothing
Except the Breath.

THE PURE SOUND

I loved Kabir at first reading
For how he sticks it to the seekers
Who insist on heaven and glory
While not watching their own feet.

I just rang my gong
And sat down in a scorching place
To bake the stupidity out
Of my restless mind.

Heaven is not a stupid thing
But insisting on it is.
I choose to refuse heaven
And listen to the ringing

Of this gong instead.
Because it brings me here,
And only here, at this time.
God and heaven will have to wait.

HEJIRA

I sit here at the end of day
In the Sonoran Desert
With a parched tongue
And a leathery palette.
The finest liquor on earth
Cannot rival the cool water
In my earthenware mug.

Mourning doves reserve songs
For the twilight hours
At each end of day light,
As they sing to me now,
With dogs barking far away,
Kids laughing on their trikes
On the sidewalk down the block.

Twenty years or more ago
In shamanic journeying,
I saw myself as an old man
Facing sundown in the desert
Where there is no place to hide,
No shelter from the all-seeing
Eyes of conscious spirit.

I came from the prairie,
Went up to the mountains
Among the holy and the crazy,
Descended for the same reason
The Desert Fathers went to Egypt,
To be found by myself at last
Listening across millions of miles.

BANKS OF THE MISSISSIPPI

The lining gave way in the coat of time.
It was eaten by the worms
Whose job it is to devour
What stands between then and now.

Gnarly trees grow along the sandy shore,
Their exposed roots, undressed by the river,
Stand all akimbo, all knees and elbows.
The scrim of dreams shimmers upriver.

Behind it are the dead whom I love:
Many relatives, the woman who married me,
And my grandfather from whom I inherited
This obsession of stuffing the litter of my life
Into poems.

For us there is no getting lost
Or having a bad love affair.
We know it is hopeless from the start—
And that brings a perverse sort of hope.

We remember everything and make it up.
If I loved you once, I always will,
And we always hope to get the last word.
If we are lucky, it is "yes".

KNOWINGNESS

Vacillating as I often do
Between doubt and belief,
I prefer doubt—but love the utter
Foolishness of a preposterous story
That could not possibly have taken place.
The mind-bending raptness,
The entertainment not bound to belief
But carried along on a dream.

We build our cathedrals for ourselves.
But the gods crave our mistakes
Because they are made passionately.
Heaven and angels sing over us
When we are wound in sleepless sheets.
They rejoice when we cry out
And when we risk everything,
Like building a ship in the desert.

Had I been back in that cultivated
Orchard with the two great trees
Growing unperturbed, untouched
In the center. I would pluck
All the pears off the branches,
Not bite just one, eat them all.
And I would not lie, but be proud
Of what I had done.

AIR, STONE, AND WATER

I have lived in cities and towns.
I have held long conversations
With beggars and madmen in back alleys,
As well as having conversed with poets
And statesmen in small cafes
And universities.
I have lived in houses, dwelt in tents,
Rented rooms where I heard fighting
Through the walls on one side,
And fucking on the other side:
I could not tell the difference at times.

Many are the tribes providing hostel
To me. And rarely have I met hostility.
I have been welcomed most of the time
But have rarely felt at home
Nor found the brother who speaks
My language, except once or twice.
But this poem does not complain
Nor does it explain my predicament.
As I try to find my face in the mirror,
I see each and every face of everyone
I have met and will ever meet.

But the one who looks back—
Who has always looked back—
The most piercingly, belongs
To another time, another place,
Neither there nor over there.
But always here in a lonesome place,
Unreflected, but not lonely. No.
No more lonely than are stars
And mountains or an ancient tree
Grown out of a promontory of rock

Living only on water and air.

WALKING WITH LISZT

Franz Liszt's "Annees de Pelerinage",
Or Years of Pilgrimage, remains somewhere
On my mind wherever my mind may go.
And lately it is on its own pilgrimage.
Franz Liszt walked away from fame, glory,
Concert halls and all their trappings
For a life of the Spirit, and its price
Of emptiness.

I have walked away, oh, so many times.
From divorce, from widowhood, from
Another divorce, from near-fatal illness
And the loss of half my body,
From moving far away, from moving far
Away yet again, from friends and family,
And the list goes on until I come upon
Everyone else on the road.

Liszt's music tells us that with thunderous
Chords and a flurry of cascading notes.
And then magnificent silence where we come
Upon the sound of our own hearts.
And so we have felt Spirit's insistent
Pounding upon our door and the rattling
Of window panes and the crashing of dishes.
Until we let it in.

PLEASE BE KIND

I used to spend my days in the deep end
Of the life pool listening intently to secrets
And shames and failures. I often disagreed.
There is no shame in living as a human being.
No secret that upon being exposed to air
Does not dry up and blow away.

I emerged a few times each day, surfacing
To the city streets of coffeeshops, book stores,
And markets. I would see someone out there
Smiling and chatting cheerfully away.
They would be in my office in an hour
Pouring out their doubts, regrets, and fears.

I never really questioned what was true.
Both Freud and the Buddha agreed
That life is difficult and full of suffering.
And a cheerful smile was simply a break.
Yet the sufferer still believed the facades of joy
They perceived along those sidewalks.

Most of us do not know what lurks in the depths
Nor the huge burden of lugging these bruised
Bodies around for a long lifetime without
Much succor. If you want advice, please ask
And listen well. Be kind to all beings.
Please be kind. Please be kind.

WHAT DO I HAVE TO SAY FOR MYSELF?

On a Saturday morning midway through
The middle of my life I sat at Java Jacks
Coffeeshop with an open journal,
An empty cup, and nothing to say.

At a nearby table, three intent people
Leaned in upon a silent, broken woman.
One man, jowls quivering,
Demanded, *What have you to say for yourself?*

A year, more or less, has come and gone.
The question lit a burning coal in my mind.

What of this self?
Shall I say, with my often self-deprecating humor
That I am a moderately successful
Shrink who would be a failing poet;
Or a sometime poet who should stick to Business?
Or perhaps a confused father,
A friend to many who don't really know him
Because he dabbles in secrets?

Or gloomily answer that perhaps this
So-called self built a perfect house
For over fifty years in which he cannot live.
Meanwhile a dreamy, inattentive boy
Has lain prone, making pictures on the floor
While humming to himself. That boy's elders
Worry what will become of him,
So sensitive and all.

But to be fair, we should say this self is
A man who listens to those who have
No witness, whose spirits are crushed

In the grinding wheels of the world.
And it's in what they say—as in the root
Of *sake*, that old word for soul—
That something mysterious happens.

There is a sea that lies beyond this
Poor man's confusion wherein drops
The moist precipitate of all his carried griefs
And wandering thoughts.

And so if all poetry
Is true dream interpretation,
Then what dreams this dreamer—
This self--
Sitting here before you
In nothing but whiteness, blankness.

AFTER PARSIFAL

Like two-natured Merlin--
Half innocent, half demon—
It is difficult to get all of me
Into one suit of clothes.

Or, like Narcissus and Goldmund,
One of me would get lost and battered
Out in the wilderness
While the other me sits calmly
At home in the garden.

Then there was rambunctious Gawain,
Roaming the entire surface of the world
For what he could never find or miss,
While Parcifal brooded in the woods.

Oh friends, I have been so pre-occupied
With what I am missing, never sitting
Still long enough to let it come to me.
Should age bring any gift,

It is this: to be ill and lame and not able
To get so lost. And so begins my awaiting
While distant stars roam overhead.
And perchance I disappear
Leaving only a whitethorn bush behind.

ODE TO TIN BUCKETS

There is something homely yet lovely
About the sound of a tin bucket
Being set down. Whether on a hard floor
Or on the ground.
A pleasingly melodic hollow sound
Perhaps our distant ancestors
Heard in the sound of the first drums
Made of hollowed logs talking
Through the forest.

It is the sound of my grandmother,
With her plain housedress
And muscled arms, finishing
Her work at day's end.
The sound of accomplished fatigue
Followed by the silence of dusk,
The fields mist with nightfall.
Could it be when we say *kick the bucket*
It is the sound of coming home.

FATHER HUNGER

The black sludge of summer's remains
Surges along the shoreline of the slough.
A coot swimming S-curves swims in
To feed of the autumnal, fecund foam.
Every man dreams of a father here,
Hidden in the reeds near the water—
Oh, so near—expecting the father to rise,
Dark swamp water dripping.

But my father is not here—he is gone.
And when he was here, he sought
His own father, who sought his own father:
They are all gone.
Who will go back in time with me?
Who will supplant this hunger?
There is no one here but the coot
And the hell diver out there
Who vanishes whenever I look up.

LONGING FOR THE CRONE
WHO LIVED NEXT DOOR

Today as I knelt upon the ground
To pull up the taproots of large
Dragon-like weeds, I sadly missed
The old crone who lived next door
When I was a child.
She was always very old,
Very bent over, with a black shawl
Draped over her rounded back.
She showed me how to get down low
With a paring knife
To pull out the whole root.

How long it has been since we last met.
I was becoming a man. She said
You used to have a sweet quiet grace
That you began to hide behind
Long stories and ironic humor.
It was time for me to go.

Fifty years on I am sad:
I miss her calm wisdom.
And I miss who I was when
We sat on long afternoons
As the sun went down
and her kerosene lamps were lit.

JESUS CHRIST

He introduced himself as Jesus Christ,
My new client who had schizophrenia,
To which he admitted suffering from.

He always took his meds on time,
Had attempted suicide many times,
And was honest about his disease.

And yet he was Jesus Christ.
That was not an issue to correct or heal.
He just thought I ought to know.

I took that in stride but had to know
If he was from Nazareth who conquered death
And whether he walked all cliffs

With temptation that angels would bear him,
Or whether he could command the world
And turn the stones to bread.

No, that was the first one, he said.
He was here to save humanity by dying
On the cross of severe mental illness.

No raising of the dead or healing the lame,
No agitation of against the State,
Or sermons from high places.

He quietly went about his days
Blessing everyone he met
And forgiving them.

I knew him for fifteen years.
We never addressed his divinity.

Bad Dreams of a Hungry Dog

I guess I followed him in my way.

METANOIA

YARMUTH

My father's father died when Dad was 38.
Just shy of my 38th, my father lay dying
In a hospital a hundred miles away.
As the afternoon unexpectedly opened
A thought slipped in to give him permission,
That it was alright, even apt, that he go.
His life was fraught with too much pain.

A week before, I put my hand on his wound
And he gave me the blessing I long needed.
When he died, the earth opened and an ocean
Of grief swallowed me and I swallowed him
Somehow, carrying him within. Two of us,
He and I within one body, but it was like that
With us. God only knows why!

Was I unconsciously refusing his death?
Or could I not accept it after being finally blest?
I went to see my therapist, I met a psychic.
I became resigned. Then I met Yarmuth.
As I lay supine on his healing table, he leaned down,
Not knowing of this particular problem, asking
Softly and gently, "Do you want your father removed?"

For two hours my body bucked and heaved
As Yarmuth reached up to his shoulder into my belly.
I retched as strands of black pitch were pulled out.
An exhausted Yarmuth fell back and dogs howled.
I was once again a sole person and Yarmuth arose,
Saying, "The quest for enlightenment
Is like the bad dreams of hungry dogs".

MOKSHA

My wife put a night light in the bathroom
Where the pastel colors shift from yellow
To orange to pink to blue then green.
And we return again
To yellow to cycle again.
Round and round colors go, and the rest of
Everything. The ancient Druids observed
And the pagans confirmed the way of these.

It is written the old Patriarch Abraham
Set about breaking that perennial wheel.
Then something utterly new could arise,
The stage for apocalyptic revolution set.

But how many revolts are launched
In that same spirit of change? From yellow
To orange and so on, over and over
Getting nowhere.
The wheels spin
And the blacktop burns, the crowds cheer.
Meanwhile the old Druids hidden in the wood
Simply shake their heads, returning to the shade.

THE BUDDHA WITHOUT HANDS

I don't know if the Buddha on my desk
Is ebony or some other tropical dark wood
But I do know he was carved in Bali.
And I do know he is very skinny
So his hip bones probably hurt
As he sits in his impeccable lotus pose.
When he had hands, he held two orbs.
The hands hold them still, but are severed.
Broken off, more likely—very old and skinny.
The Buddha knows more about these things
Than you and I will ever know: old age,
Sickness, and death. Impermanence, too.
He would admonish me throw the hands away,
But attached as I am to things like hands,
Especially the Buddha's hands, I keep them.
When you are compassionate, people give you
Their breaking hearts. You must be able
To deftly, lightly, hold these things.
That is why I keep the Buddha's hands.

GOING TOO FAR

This time you've gone too far!
How many times have I heard that
Admonishment, and not only in youth.
If something is good or funny or exciting,
Why not keep going to the edge, and over.
Yes, I've known my share of shame
If only for the rest of the day.
And I've known heartache and loss
As my impetuous heart kept overflowing
Much as the Red River in Spring.
Perhaps that is the tuition we pay
To enter the universe of poetry.
As an elder poet told me once
I could either be poet or a saint—
Goldmund or Narcissus—but not both.

When Eve bade Adam take a bite
Of the forbidden pear, it was a set up.
The trick was always to eat them all
And not lie about it: be proud
As I have been of my catastrophe.
And here I sit amid my stories
Of defeat, comedy, and victory
Amid this overgrown garden.
I am as harmless as a dove by now,
But wise as a serpent.

SITTING DOWN AFTER STANDING

Sitting down after a lifetime of standing up
It is time for other exercise
Not of the body, or of the limbs,
Or on the surfaces of this world.

Some neglected spirit now calls for attention.
The eternal but invisible inside me
Needs to come out to play, Soaring
Through seven atmospheres.

I have read most of the scriptures
And they came down to an admixture
Of twenty six letters, ten digits, on paper.
Lots and lots of paper, and ink.

And I have chanted till dawn,
Bringing the sun up with my devotion,
Have drummed till my fingers bled,
Danced till the sun went down again.

I have not found God up there,
Or out there, not even in there.
What I found was myself still standing
And laughing. And now I will sit down.

TIKKUN OLAM

Lately I have been dreaming while awake.
An old Rabbi appears in his dusty black clothes,
Long grey beard, long forelocks descending
From beneath his yarmulke. Carrying the Torah,
Of course, wearily up a steep dusty road.
He motions for me to follow.

When something like this happens
And keeps happening, we must pay attention
However baffling: there is no trace Jewishness
That anyone in my family will admit.
But I have my doubts, as did my father.
Why the resolute Lutheran dogma without faith
And the strong refusal of circumcision?

We carry all human history in our souls,
And I hold more than few libraries of Judaica.
But conversion is not the rabbi's goal.
He has witnessed more than a human should.
And he is old. He climbs the hill—walking away?
Toward heaven or another world to heal?

Whether to follow or not, to bid him stay,
Is not the issue: I am going nonetheless.
Many times, we walk together of late,
Perhaps in brotherhood, sharing weary tears.
I would carry him if I could. He is ahead
But nevertheless carrying me.

ORGANIZATION MAN

God and devil walk along one day
Through the Creation they each
Know well from their own advantage.
They've known each other a long time
And they've had their disagreements
And made a wager or two.
But God stopped keeping score
About who owes whom.

There is a shining object on the ground
Which God picks up fondly.
Says, "Would you look at that!"
And the devil implores him,
"What is it? What is it?"
To which God says, "This, my friend,
Is Truth," and gives it to the devil
To organize.

And so it is, or so it seems,
And sometimes God finds himself
Uncertain about the existence of God.
That is a joke they told in heaven
Before I was born while angels
Chuckled and nodded their heads.
When I repeat it down here,
Many are too terrified to laugh.

AT THE STROKE OF MIDNIGHT

My clock has struck a certain note
At a certain time in my life.
According to Yeats, my war
On you should have begun.
But I have wrestled with your angels
And fought your enemies
My whole life long.
All I accomplished is exhaustion.

Have I been angry? Have I rebelled?
Have I half-heartedly denied you?
Of course. And of course, I came crawling
Back, with the blood of your son on my hands.

Why is it you answer me,
When you do, in the most baffling ways?
Most of humanity wails your name
From the ditches of despair
All day and all night long.
And yet you turn a deaf ear!

I have been picking your lock
Trying to get into your heaven
Without dying. And yet when I give up,
Fatigued, sweating, only then can I bless
My life, its imponderable mystery
Of the improbability of anything—
Any thing. What was it
Yeats wrote?
At the stroke of midnight
You shall win.

NOT TAKING BAD ADVICE

I was told at twenty I had to choose
Between being a poet or a saint.
I sat there in my soft shoulder-length hair,
Fuzzy start of a beard,
And an OM medallion around my neck.
Part anarchist and part novitiate
In the seminary of poetic devotion
Seeming to have stepped out of Hesse.

It was my prof, after all, who was stuck
Between Narcissus and Goldmund
While I lit out fast without direction:
When you're blazing a trail, dear,
There are no directions home
Nor any instructions for the wilderness.
And I had not yet come across the embers
Of fires lit by Rumi, Hafez, and Kabir.

Do not let anyone tell you saints are pure:
They are ragged, irascible, and whole.
And often crazy—meaning the glaze coating
Of the shiny people is cracked by heat and light.
The untamed, wild, and extravagant souls
Somehow avoided the normal amputation.
I have spent the better part of my life
Searching among the cast offs for myself.

Early on in my wandering pilgrimage
I awoke from a dream convinced
The Grail lay dented and dusty on a bank
Amid a myriad of junk and trash
Down among the industrial waste
On the shores of the Mississippi.
Or confused among the rags and bones

In the Salvation Army stores.

Now, nearly fifty years on, cast off myself,
I am an assemblage of contradictions
But nearly whole at last, having glimpsed
The Grail in passing a few times
And caught a smile from the King
Of Grace and Beauty at long last.
Am I making any sense? It is alright:
I am drunk and this is the edge of the roof.

PICKING GOD'S LOCK

I have been picking God's lock
Ever since I learned about religion.
I sat at the knees of ministers, priests,
Rabbis, and Eastern gurus of all stripes.
The more I studied and the harder I prayed,
The more my suffering increased.
Now I am on the cusp of old age
And am a miserable old man--
Too young and lucky to be
So old and unhappy.
And I am troubled by dying.

But what is dying except just stepping
Up and out of this heap of heavy flesh,
Letting the winds of ether sweep me up?
Or I could remain in this barroom—
This dusty, musky, and dark tavern
We call the real world, repeating my tales,
Being fleeced and robbed and cheated,
Forgetting that Soul wants it all taken away.
And where is God in all this? Shaking
His cosmic head while I run back to sort
Through all my old poems.

LIGHTING CANDLES

When I first came here,
Oh, so long ago in another time,
It was the songs and drums of Africa
Which drew me to my first parents
In a hut on the Serengeti.
I knew nothing of cruelty--
Not betrayal nor poverty.

Thousands of years later
On the prairies of Minnesota,
I landed in the aproned laps
Of Scandinavian immigrants
With sweet milk on my tongue.

I was given St. Jerome's name,
Pointing the way to the pulpit
And the altar, my grandfather smiling
From the dark oaken pews
Of the Norwegian Lutheran Church.

I began to argue with God
Decades later, fooled by the hypocrisy
That fools us all into argument.
We lived as neighbors
For many, many years,
Nodding on the way to the car.
I shouted at him at times
To keep it down and let me be,
Although I heard nothing but music.
And he paid my rent.

The other night I dreamed
An old beggar woman on the street--
Crippled, toothless--called out to me

Saying, "Praise God!"
And kept repeating it until
I joined her exuberantly.

Then she asked, "Jere, why
Do you persist in saying you know nothing
About God? Do you not know
You are lighting candles on the path
Up the hill to the temple all this time.
The power may be out,
A hurricane may be blowing,
But you are as stubborn,
And as cunning, as Jacob."
I awoke, and then I wept.

A LOVE STORY

You put me here in the time of mass extinction,
Grew me up under a radioactive fungal cloud,
Watched me witness the plagues of feudal despair
And willful, entrenched ignorance.
It is amazing I have even a shred of trust, but
Tatters of it still hang in the air between us.

People argue all day and night about you
But I was never articulate at your defense,
Unable to truly say what I mean till now.
But there may not be much time and I see
Finally that your holiness shines in everything--
A consciousness, however frail: ours.

A bright mind can shine like scorching sun,
But without Soul, it leaves a barren wasteland.
And a wandering Soul without strong mind
Leads to aimless superstition and folly.
You watched me play both games and lose
Yet the stakes are high and I am broke.

I took the ladder given to me, and the one
I stole in my unworthiness. You called me
And I climbed it weary rung by weary rung.

Who could have known you were the ladder?
And now I am back at the bottom where
It starts—in the longing of my lonely heart.

Would that I could have spared myself
The years of self-abnegation and flagellation,
Or Martin Luther torture and Siddhartha
Binge and purge. But then, what wisdom?
There lies little left to do but simply love you,

And, as your rabbis say, be a good person.

THE VOICE OF WATER

You have the voice of water
Gathered in sunlight.
I put my hand in the urn
And felt no moisture.
I do not hear your voice.

In the barking of dogs,
In the rattles of windowpanes,
In the squeak of earth beneath feet,
Your song is lost,
Although every wooden thing aches.

The candle light grows dim,
Dimmer in the night's hidden light.
No passage of darkness is noticed.
When I am no longer called by my name,
I will hear you call.

EVERY MORNING

Every morning I wake up with a body
Full of new blood.
Where I was yesterday was millions
Of miles away in the universe.
And in my sleep I went across time
And across the land of the dead.
That's enough travel for now.

I am one who has come a long way
To my destiny only to forget why he came.
So I keep on walking.
The world is full of amnesiacs like me.
That is why Christ told the Gnostics:
"As far as you can go, stand there!"
The trick is to stay put for forty years.

www.ingramcontent.com/pod-product-compliance
Lightning Source LLC
LaVergne TN
LVHW041541060526
838200LV00037B/1092